Jason - Thomp...
Nome...

Bring her to T
pre-arranged
Meth Church
day?
Closed casket
J. wanted Visitation?
(clothes)

!ML - not open casket
pictures of her

Claire -
J call Sat - in Bosnie
gave Jim# Debbie # Sherry #
Claire told Jim to call
Police.
closed casket - no Visitation

Marc - not coming
Tom Mekes - text
Carol Y, Jill - "
Suzanne B "

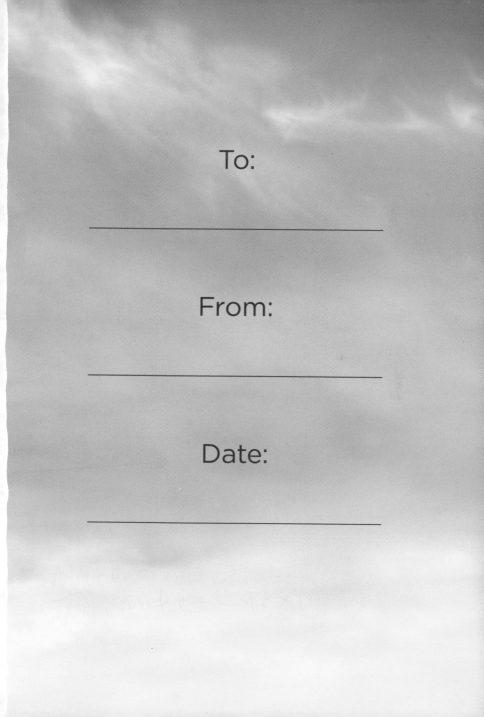

To:

_____

From:

_____

Date:

_____

REFLECTIONS
ON THE
LORD'S PRAYER

Reflections on the Lord's Prayer

Copyright © 2009, 2015

ISBN 978-0-3103-4982-2

Interior Photography: © Shutterstock: pages 1-8, 11-14, 16-18, 21-22, 24-25, 27-32, 35-38, 41-43, 45-46, 48-50, 53-56, 58-61, 63-64, 67-69, 71, 73, 75-76, 78-79, 81-82, 85-88, 91, 93-96, 99, 101, 103, 105-106, 109-114, 116-119, 121, 123-124, 126-127, 129, 131, 133, 135, 137-138, 140-142, 145-146, 149, 151-153, 155, 157-160

Printed in China

15 16 17 18 19 20 /TIMS/ 22 21 20 19 18 17 16 15 14 13 12 11 10 9 8 7 6 5 4 3 2 1

Contents

LORD, TEACH US TO PRAY

One day Jesus was praying in a certain place. When
he finished, one of his disciples said to him, "Lord,
teach us to pray, just as John taught his disciples."

—LUKE 11:1

The Lord's Prayer

"This, then, is how you should pray:
'Our Father in heaven,
hallowed be your name,
your kingdom come,
your will be done
    on earth as it is in heaven.
Give us today our daily bread.
Forgive us our debts,
    as we also have forgiven our debtors.
And lead us not into temptation,
but deliver us from the evil one.
For yours is the kingdom and the power and the
    glory forever.
    Amen.'" *

—Matthew 6:9–13

---

* The final sentence is included only as a footnote in many modern
Bible translations, because it is missing from some of the ancient
manuscripts. However, since the first century AD, followers of
Jesus have commonly used these words to end the Lord's Prayer.

Introduction

After having denounced showy and meaningless prayers, Christ introduced a splendid short prayer of His own. With it, He instructed us on how to pray and what we should pray for. He gave us a prayer that touches upon a variety of needs. By themselves, these needs should compel us to approach God daily with these few easily remembered words. No one can excuse himself by saying he doesn't know how to pray or what to pray for.

The Lord's Prayer is the finest prayer that anyone could have ever thought up or that was ever sent from heaven. Because God the Father gave His Son the words for the prayer and sent Him to introduce it, we know beyond a doubt that His prayer pleases the Father immensely.

—Martin Luther

Let us have a great esteem for the Lord's Prayer; let it be the model and pattern of all our prayers.

—Thomas Watson

So the disciples learned from the Lord's own mouth the several petitions of that prayer which we still call "The Lord's." And we still pray it. Believers all around the globe pray the elegant, elemental, comprehensive, bold and humble prayer—mostly in the words preserved in Matthew 6:9–13.

As we prayed with the psalmist, and with the faithful of the Church, so we may pray with Jesus. He gave us these words to make our own.

But he also gave us the remarkable insight that words of prayer may match prayerful deeds, until we have begun to live *a life of prayer*! It is this which is mostly missed about his teaching. He taught His disciples the same prayer at two times and in two ways; for He who said, "Pray, 'Our Father who art in heaven . . . thy will be done,'" then went forth and actually performed his prayer, did it, enacted it, accomplished the same thing in His body and soul.

After the Master had taught the lesson of prayer, He went out and *became* the lesson.

—WALT WANGERIN

The Model Prayer of our Lord, called familiarly "the Lord's Prayer," is the universal prayer, because it is peculiarly adapted to all men everywhere in all circumstances in all times of need. It can be put in the mouths of all people in all nations, and in all times. It is a model of praying which needs no amendment nor alteration for every family, people and nation.

—E. M. BOUNDS

PREFACE

OUR FATHER IN HEAVEN

What does this preface to the Lord's Prayer teach us?

The preface of the Lord's Prayer, which is "Our Father which art in heaven," teacheth us to draw near to God with all holy reverence and confidence, as children to a father, able and ready to help us; and that we should pray with and for others.

—Westminster Shorter Catechism

Those who can say, "Our Father which art in heaven," are something more than God's creatures: they have been adopted into His family. He has taken them out of the old black family in which they were born; He

has washed them, and cleansed them, and given them
a new name and a new spirit, and made them "heirs of
God, and joint-heirs with Christ"; and all this of His
own free, sovereign, unmerited, distinguishing grace.

—CHARLES H. SPURGEON

OUR FATHER

What does it mean to address God as "Our Father"?

Right at the beginning of the prayer, with the word
"Our Father," Jesus reminds us of what God demands
and promises. God insists that we give Him the
respect, honor, and reverence He deserves, just as
earthly fathers expect this from their children. Also,
God the Father wants us to trust that He will meet
our needs. We are overjoyed to be His children
through Christ. And so, because we trust that He will
give us what He promised, we can pray to Him with
confidence, in the name of Christ, our Lord.

—MARTIN LUTHER

And thanks be to the mercy of Him who requires this
of us, that He should be our Father—a relationship
which can be brought about by no expenditure of
ours, but solely by God's good will.

—ST. AUGUSTINE

Princes on earth give themselves titles expressing their greatness, as "High and Mighty." God might have done so, and expressed Himself thus, "Our King of glory, our Judge," but He gives himself another title, "Our Father," an expression of love and condescension. That He might encourage us to pray to Him, He represents Himself under the sweet notion of a father. The name Jehovah carries majesty in it; the name Father carries mercy in it.

—THOMAS WATSON

At the very beginning of our prayer Christ wants to kindle in us what is basic to our prayer—the childlike awe and trust that God through Christ has become our Father. Our fathers do not refuse us the things of this life; God our Father will even less refuse to give us what we ask in faith.

—HEIDELBERG CATECHISM

Christ taught us also to approach the Father in His name. That is our passport. It is in His name that we are to make petitions known.

—E. M. BOUNDS

Those who are led by the Spirit of God are sons of God. For you did not receive a spirit that makes you a slave again to fear, but you received the Spirit of sonship. And by him we cry, "*Abba*, Father." The Spirit himself testifies with our spirit that we are God's children.

—ROMANS 8:14–16

With the tongue we praise our Lord and Father.

—JAMES 3:9

Our fellowship is with the Father and with his Son,
Jesus Christ.

—1 JOHN 1:3

How great is the love the Father has lavished on us,
that we should be called children of God! And that is
what we are!

—1 JOHN 3:1

Praise be to the God and Father of our Lord Jesus
Christ, who has blessed us in the heavenly realms
with every spiritual blessing in Christ.

—EPHESIANS 1:3

There is one body and one Spirit—just as you were
called to one hope when you were called—one Lord,
one faith, one baptism; one God and Father of all,
who is over all and through all and in all.

—EPHESIANS 4:4–6

I will be a Father to you,
and you will be my sons and daughters,
says the Lord Almighty.

—2 CORINTHIANS 6:18

Every good and perfect gift is from above, coming
down from the Father of the heavenly lights, who
does not change like shifting shadows. He chose
to give us birth through the word of truth, that we
might be a kind of firstfruits of all he created.

—JAMES 1:17–18

Sing and make music in your heart to the Lord,
always giving thanks to God the Father for
everything, in the name of our Lord Jesus Christ.

—EPHESIANS 5:19–20

"Which of you, if his son asks for bread, will give him a
stone? Or if he asks for a fish, will give him a snake? If
you, then, though you are evil, know how to give good
gifts to your children, how much more will your Father
in heaven give good gifts to those who ask him!"

—MATTHEW 7:9–11

In Heaven

*Why is it important to acknowledge
our Father is in heaven?*

> God is said to be in heaven, not because He is so
> included there as if He were nowhere else; for "the
> heaven of heavens cannot contain thee" (1 Kings 8:27).
> But the meaning is, that He is chiefly resident in what
> the apostle calls "the third heaven," where He reveals
> His glory most to saints and angels (2 Corinthians 12:2).
>
> —Thomas Watson

> Heaven is a place of perfect purity, and we must
> therefore lift up pure hands, must study to sanctify
> His name, who is the Holy One, and dwells in that
> holy place. He is a Father, and therefore we may come
> to Him with boldness, but a Father in heaven, and
> therefore we must come with reverence.
>
> —Matthew Henry

> The words "in heaven" teach us not to think of God's
> heavenly majesty as something earthly, and to expect
> everything for body and soul from His almighty power.
>
> —Heidelberg Catechism

Yet give attention to your servant's prayer and his
plea for mercy, O LORD my God. Hear the cry and the
prayer that your servant is praying in your presence
this day. . . . Hear from heaven, your dwelling place,
and when you hear, forgive.

—1 KINGS 8:28, 30

The priests and the Levites stood to bless the people,
and God heard them, for their prayer reached heaven,
his holy dwelling place.

—2 CHRONICLES 30:27

From heaven the LORD looks down
    and sees all mankind;
from his dwelling place he watches
    all who live on earth—
he who forms the hearts of all,
    who considers everything they do.

—PSALM 33:13–15

The LORD has established his throne in heaven,
    and his kingdom rules over all.

—PSALM 103:19

"Do not I fill heaven and earth?" declares the LORD.
"Am I only a God nearby," declares the LORD, "and
not a God far away? Can anyone hid in secret places
so that I cannot see him?" declares the LORD.

—JEREMIAH 23:23–24

I lift up my eyes to you,
  to you whose throne is in heaven.

—PSALM 123:1

The LORD is exalted over all the nations,
  his glory above the heavens.
Who is like the LORD our God,
  the One who sits enthroned on high,
who stoops down to look
  on the heavens and the earth?

—PSALM 113:4–6

The God who made the world and everything in it
is the Lord of heaven and earth and does not live in
temples built by hands. And he is not served by human
hands, as if he needed anything, because he himself
gives all men life and breath and everything else.

—ACTS 17:24–25

After [Jesus] said this, he was taken up before their
very eyes, and a cloud hid him from their sight.

They were looking intently up into the sky as he
was going, when suddenly two men dressed in white
stood beside them. "Men of Galilee," they said, "why
do you stand here looking into the sky? This same
Jesus, who has been taken from you into heaven, will
come back in the same way you have seen him go into
heaven."

—ACTS 1:9–11

He ascended into heaven and is seated at the right
hand of God the Father Almighty.

—THE APOSTLES' CREED

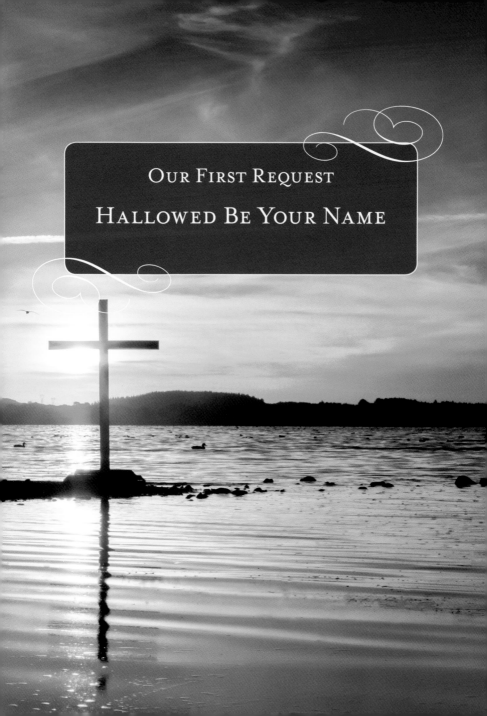

Hallowed Be Your Name

What do we mean when we ask that
God's name be hallowed?

The first petition is that God's name be hallowed.
Though all ungodly men should break out with their
sacrilegious license, the holiness of God's name still
shines. We should wish God to have the honor He
deserves; men should never speak or think of Him
without the highest reverence. To this is opposed the
profanity that has always been too common and even
today is abroad in the world. Hence the need of this
petition, which ought to have been superfluous if
even a little godliness existed among us.

—John Calvin

When we say, "Hallowed be Thy name," we do not
mean that God's name is not holy, but we ask that
men may treat it as a holy thing.

—St. Augustine

This means, help us to really know you, to bless,
worship, and praise You for all Your works and for all
that shines forth from them: Your almighty power,
wisdom, kindness, justice, mercy, and truth. And it
means, help us to direct all our living—what we think,
say, and do—so that Your name will never be blas-
phemed because of us but always honored and praised.

—Heidelberg Catechism

In the first petition, which is "Hallowed be thy name," we pray that God would enable us, and others, to glorify Him in all that whereby He maketh Himself known; and that He would dispose all things to His own glory.

—WESTMINSTER SHORTER CATECHISM

"You shall not misuse the name of the LORD your God, for the LORD will not hold anyone guiltless who misuses his name."

—EXODUS 20:7

"Do not swear falsely by my name and so profane the name of your God. I am the LORD."

—LEVITICUS 19:12

Put away perversity from your mouth;
    keep corrupt talk far from your lips.

—PROVERBS 4:24

"Do not profane my holy name. I must be acknowledged as holy by the Israelites. I am the LORD, who makes you holy and who brought you out of Egypt to be your God. I am the LORD."

—LEVITICUS 22:32–33

Do not let any unwholesome talk come out of your mouths, but only what is helpful for building others up according to their needs, that it may benefit those who listen. And do not grieve the Holy Spirit of God, with whom you were sealed for the day of redemption.

—Ephesians 4:29–30

"Among those who approach me
    I will show myself holy;
in the sight of all the people
    I will be honored."

—Leviticus 10:3

Glory in his holy name;
    let the hearts of those who seek the Lord rejoice.

—1 Chronicles 16:10

Save us, O Lord our God,
    and gather us from the nations,
that we may give thanks to your holy name
    and glory in your praise.

—Psalm 106:47

Then those who feared the LORD talked with each other, and the LORD listened and heard. A scroll of remembrance was written in his presence concerning those who feared the LORD and honored his name.

—MALACHI 3:16

Who will not fear you, O Lord,
    and bring glory to your name?
For you alone are holy.
All nations will come
    and worship before you,
for your righteous acts have been revealed.

—REVELATION 15:4

By what name is God called?

A name which is above every name—dignity and
majesty superior to every creature.

—JOHN WESLEY

The consideration of His name, or names, is worthy of regard, because they serve to lead into some
knowledge of His nature and perfections. From all
these names of God we learn that God is the eternal,
immutable, and almighty Being, the Being of beings,
self-existent, and self-sufficient, and the object of
religious worship and adoration.

—JOHN GILL

Moses said to God, "Suppose I go to the Israelites and say to them, 'The God of your fathers has sent me to you,' and they ask me, 'What is his name?' Then what shall I tell them?"

God said to Moses, "I AM WHO I AM. This is what you are to say to the Israelites: 'I AM has sent me to you.'"

—EXODUS 3:13–14

Then the LORD came down in the cloud and stood there with him and proclaimed his name, the LORD.

—EXODUS 34:5

And he will be called
    Wonderful Counselor, Mighty God,
    Everlasting Father, Prince of Peace.

—ISAIAH 9:6

I am the LORD; that is my name!

—ISAIAH 42:8

Our Redeemer—the LORD Almighty is his name—
    is the Holy One of Israel.

—ISAIAH 47:4

This is what the LORD says,
he who appoints the sun
    to shine by day,
who decrees the moon and stars
    to shine by night,
who stirs up the sea
    so that its waves roar—
    the LORD Almighty is his name.

—JEREMIAH 31:35

No one is like you, O Lord;
    you are great,
    and your name is mighty in power.

—Jeremiah 10:6

But the angel said to her, "Do not be afraid, Mary, you have found favor with God. You will be with child and give birth to a son, and you are to give him the name Jesus. He will be great and will be called the Son of the Most High."

—Luke 1:30–32

Then Daniel praised the God of heaven and said:
    "Praise be to the name of God for ever and ever;
    wisdom and power are his."

—Daniel 2:19–20

Therefore God exalted him to the highest place
    and gave him the name that is above every name,
that at the name of Jesus every knee should bow,
    in heaven and on earth and under the earth,
and every tongue confess that Jesus Christ is Lord,
    to the glory of God the Father.

—Philippians 2:9–11

"For I am the Lord your God,
    who churns up the sea so that its waves roar—
    the Lord Almighty is his name."

—Isaiah 51:15

Today in the town of David a Savior has been born to you; he is Christ the Lord.

—Luke 2:11

Simon Peter answered, "You are the Christ, the Son of the living God."

—Matthew 16:16

"Therefore go and make disciples of all nations, baptizing them in the name of the Father and of the Son and of the Holy Spirit."

—Matthew 28:19

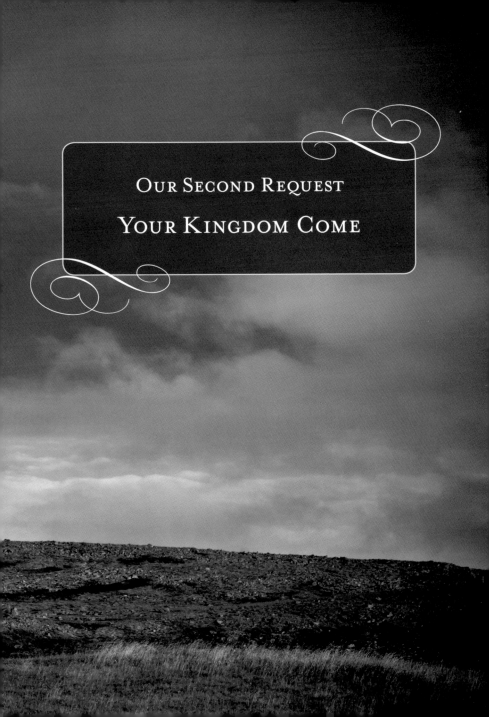

OUR SECOND REQUEST

YOUR KINGDOM COME

Your Kingdom Come

What does this request mean?

"Your kingdom come" means, rule us by Your Word and Spirit in such a way that more and more we submit to You. Keep Your church strong, and add to it. Destroy the devil's work; destroy every force which revolts against You and every conspiracy against Your Word. Do this until Your kingdom is so complete and perfect that in it You are all in all.

—Heidelberg Catechism

"But seek first his kingdom and his righteousness, and all these things will be given to you as well."

—Matthew 6:33

Your Kingdom Come

What do we know about God's kingdom?
The kingdom of God is within us.

God's kingdom is nothing but godliness, chastity, purity, gentleness, tenderness, and kindness. His kingdom is full of every virtue and grace. . . . This should be our first and foremost desire. We are saved only when God reigns in us, and we become His kingdom.

—Martin Luther

The central point of the kingdom of Jesus Christ is a personal relationship with Him, not public usefulness to others.

—Oswald Chambers

Jesus said, "My kingdom is not of this world. If it were, my servants would fight to prevent my arrest by the Jews. But now my kingdom is from another place."

—John 18:36

"And do not set your heart on what you will eat or drink; do not worry about it. For the pagan world runs after all such things, and your Father knows that you need them. But seek his kingdom, and these things will be given to you as well."

—Luke 12:29–31

For the kingdom of God is not a matter of eating and drinking, but of righteousness, peace and joy in the Holy Spirit, because anyone who serves Christ in this way is pleasing to God and approved by men.

—ROMANS 14:17–18

For the kingdom of God is not a matter of talk but of power.

—1 CORINTHIANS 4:20

You are witnesses, and so is God, of how holy, righteous and blameless we were among you who believed. For you know that we dealt with each of you as a father deals with his own children, encouraging, comforting and urging you to live lives worthy of God, who calls you into his kingdom and glory.

—1 THESSALONIANS 2:10–12

Once, having been asked by the Pharisees when the kingdom of God would come, Jesus replied, "The kingdom of God does not come with your careful observation, nor will people say, 'Here it is,' or 'There it is,' because the kingdom of God is within you."

—LUKE 17:20–21

"The time has come," [Jesus] said. "The kingdom of God is near. Repent and believe the good news!"

—MARK 1:15

Then Jesus asked, "What is the kingdom of God like? What shall I compare it to? It is like a mustard seed, which a man took and planted in his garden. It grew and became a tree, and the birds of the air perched in its branches."

Again he asked, "What shall I compare the kingdom of God to? It is like yeast that a woman took and mixed into a large amount of flour until it worked all through the dough."

—LUKE 13:18–21

How do we enter this kingdom?

In reply Jesus declared, "I tell you the truth, no one can see the kingdom of God unless he is born again."

—JOHN 3:3

Jesus answered, "I tell you the truth, no one can enter the kingdom of God unless he is born of water and the Spirit. Flesh gives birth to flesh, but the Spirit gives birth to spirit."

—JOHN 3:5–6

People were bringing little children to Jesus to have him touch them, but the disciples rebuked them. When Jesus saw this, he was indignant. He said to them, "Let the little children come to me, and do not hinder them, for the kingdom of God belongs to such as these. I tell you the truth, anyone who will not receive the kingdom of God like a little child will never enter it." And he took the children in his arms, put his hands on them and blessed them.

—MARK 10:13–16

What else do we know about God's kingdom?
The kingdom of God is in the future.

> In the second petition, which is "Thy kingdom come,"
> we pray that Satan's kingdom may be destroyed; and
> that the kingdom of grace may be advanced, ourselves
> and others brought into it, and kept in it; and that the
> kingdom of glory may be hastened.
>
> —WESTMINSTER SHORTER CATECHISM

> Thy kingdom come—may Thy kingdom of grace
> come quickly, and swallow up all the kingdoms of the
> earth: may all mankind, receiving Thee, O Christ, for
> their king, truly believing in Thy name, be filled with
> righteousness, and peace, and joy; with holiness and
> happiness, till they are removed hence into Thy king-
> dom of glory, to reign with Thee for ever and ever.
>
> —JOHN WESLEY

> In the time of those kings, the God of heaven will
> set up a kingdom that will never be destroyed, nor
> will it be left to another people. It will crush all those
> kingdoms and bring them to an end, but it will itself
> endure forever.
>
> —DANIEL 2:44

Then King Darius wrote to all the peoples, nations and men of every language throughout the land:

"May you prosper greatly!

"I issue a decree that in every part of my kingdom people must fear and reverence the God of Daniel.

"For he is the living God
and he endures forever;
his kingdom will not be destroyed,
his dominion will never end.
He rescues and he saves;
he performs signs and wonders
in the heavens and on the earth.
He has rescued Daniel
from the power of the lions."

—Daniel 6:25–27

The Lord God will give him the throne of his father David, and he will reign over the house of Jacob forever; his kingdom will never end.

—Luke 1:32–33

Therefore, my brothers, be all the more eager to make your calling and election sure. For if you do these things, you will never fall, and you will receive a rich welcome into the eternal kingdom of our Lord and Savior Jesus Christ.

—2 Peter 1:10–11

"There will be signs in the sun, moon and stars. On the earth, nations will be in anguish and perplexity at the roaring and tossing of the sea. Men will faint from terror, apprehensive of what is coming on the world, for the heavenly bodies will be shaken. At that time they will see the Son of Man coming in a cloud with power and great glory. When these things begin to take place, stand up and lift up your heads, because your redemption is drawing near."

He told them this parable: "Look at the fig tree and all the trees. When they sprout leaves, you can see for yourselves and know that summer is near. Even so, when you see these things happening, you know that the kingdom of God is near."

—LUKE 21:25–31

But about the Son he says,
"Your throne, O God, will last for ever and ever,
and righteousness will be the scepter of your kingdom."

—Hebrews 1:8

Listen, my dear brothers: has not God chosen those
who are poor in the eyes of the world to be rich in
faith and to inherit the kingdom he promised those
who love him?

—James 2:5

In the presence of God and of Christ Jesus, who will judge the living and the dead, and in view of his appearing and his kingdom, I give you this charge: Preach the Word; be prepared in season and out of season; correct, rebuke and encourage—with great patience and careful instruction.

—2 TIMOTHY 4:1–2

"For the Son of Man is going to come in his Father's glory with his angels, and then he will reward each person according to what he has done. I tell you the truth, some who are standing here will not taste death before they see the Son of Man coming in his kingdom."

—MATTHEW 16:27–28

The seventh angel sounded his trumpet, and there were loud voices in heaven, which said:
"The kingdom of the world has become the kingdom of our Lord and of his Christ,
and he will reign for ever and ever."

—REVELATION 11:15

Then I heard a loud voice in heaven say:
"Now have come the salvation and the power
and the kingdom of our God,
and the authority of his Christ.
For the accuser of our brothers,
who accuses them before our God day and night,
has been hurled down."

—REVELATION 12:10

Our Third Request

Your Will Be Done on Earth As It Is in Heaven

Your Will Be Done on Earth As It Is in Heaven

What does this third request mean?

> The kingdom of God is a society upon earth where God's will is as perfectly done as it is in heaven.
>
> —William Barclay

> We are therefore bidden to desire that, just as in heaven nothing is done apart from God's good pleasure, and the angels dwell together in all peace and uprightness, the earth be in like manner subject to such a rule, with all arrogance and wickedness brought to an end.
>
> —John Calvin

"Your will be done on earth as it is in heaven" means, help us and all people to reject our own wills and to obey Your will without any back talk. Your will alone is good. Help us one and all to carry out the work we are called to, as willingly and faithfully as the angels in heaven.

—HEIDELBERG CATECHISM

In the third petition, which is "Thy will be done in earth, as it is in heaven," we pray that God, by His grace, would make us able and willing to know, obey, and submit to His will in all things, as the angels do in heaven.

—WESTMINSTER SHORTER CATECHISM

YOUR WILL BE DONE ON EARTH

How can we do God's will on earth?

We make Christ but a titular Prince, if we call Him King, and do not do His will: having prayed that He may rule us, we pray that we may in every thing be ruled by Him.

—MATTHEW HENRY

Be very careful, then, how you live—not as unwise but as wise, making the most of every opportunity, because the days are evil. Therefore do not be foolish, but understand what the Lord's will is.

—EPHESIANS 5:15–17

So do not throw away your confidence; it will be richly rewarded. You need to persevere so that when you have done the will of God, you will receive what he has promised.

—HEBREWS 10:35–36

I desire to do your will, O my God;
    your law is within my heart.

—PSALM 40:8

Teach me to do your will,
    for you are my God;
may your good Spirit
    lead me on level ground.

—PSALM 143:10

Grace and peace to you from God our Father and the Lord Jesus Christ, who gave himself for our sins to rescue us from the present evil age, according to the will of our God and Father, to whom be glory for ever and ever. Amen.

—GALATIANS 1:3–5

For this reason, since the day we heard about you, we have not stopped praying for you and asking God to fill you with the knowledge of his will through all spiritual wisdom and understanding. And we pray this in order that you may live a life worthy of the Lord and may please him in every way: bearing fruit in every good work, growing in the knowledge of God.

—COLOSSIANS 1:9–10

Therefore, since Christ suffered in his body, arm yourselves also with the same attitude, because he who has suffered in his body is done with sin. As a result, he does not live the rest of his earthly life for evil human desires, but rather for the will of God.

—1 Peter 4:1–2

So then, those who suffer according to God's will should commit themselves to their faithful Creator and continue to do good.

—1 Peter 4:19

It is better, if it is God's will, to suffer for doing good than for doing evil.

—1 Peter 3:17

Give thanks in all circumstance, for this is God's will for you in Christ Jesus.

—1 Thessalonians 5:18

Do not conform any longer to the pattern of this world, but be transformed by the renewing of your mind. Then you will be able to test and approve what God's will is—his good, pleasing and perfect will.

—Romans 12:2

The world and its desires pass away, but the man who does the will of God lives forever.

—1 JOHN 2:17

[Jesus said,] "Father, if you are willing, take this cup from me; yet not my will, but yours be done."

—LUKE 22:42

"Not everyone who says to me, 'Lord, Lord,' will enter the kingdom of heaven, but only he who does the will of my Father who is in heaven."

—MATTHEW 7:21

Your Will Be Done . . . As It Is in Heaven

How is God's will done in heaven?

Heaven is by name compared to earth, for the angels,
as is said in the psalm, willingly obey God, and are
intent upon carrying out His commands.

—John Calvin

We pray that earth may be made more like heaven
by the observance of God's will (this earth, which,
through the prevalency of Satan's will, has become so
near akin to hell), and that saints may be made more
like the holy angels in their devotion and obedience.

—Matthew Henry

The Lord has established his throne in heaven,
    and his kingdom rules over all.
Praise the Lord, you his angels,
    you mighty ones who do his bidding,
    who obey his word.
Praise the Lord, all his heavenly hosts,
    you his servants who do his will.
Praise the Lord, all his works
    everywhere in his dominion.
Praise the Lord, O my soul.

—Psalm 103:19–22

Our Fourth Request

Give Us This Day Our Daily Bread

GIVE US THIS DAY OUR DAILY BREAD

What does this request mean?

The good things of this life are the gifts of God; He is the donor of all our blessings. "Give Us." Not faith only, but food is the gift of God; not daily grace only is from God, but "daily bread"; every good thing comes from God. All we have is from the hand of God's royal bounty; we have nothing but what He gives us out of His storehouse; we cannot have one bit of bread but from God.

—THOMAS WATSON

In the fourth petition, which is "Give us this day our daily bread," we pray that of God's free gift we may receive a competent portion of the good things of this life, and enjoy His blessing with them.

—WESTMINSTER SHORTER CATECHISM

"Give us today our daily bread" means do take care of all our physical needs so that we come to know that You are the only source of everything good, and that neither our work and worry nor Your gifts can do us any good without Your blessing. And so help us to give up our trust in creatures and to put trust in You alone.

—HEIDELBERG CATECHISM

Give Us This Day . . .

What does it mean that God gives it to us?

We beg of God to *give* it us, not sell it us, nor lend it us, but *give* it. The greatest of men must be beholden to the mercy of God their *daily bread*. We pray that God would give us *this day*; which teaches us to renew the desire of our souls toward God, as the wants of our bodies are renewed; as duly as the day comes, we must pray to our heavenly Father, and reckon we could as well go a day without meat, as without prayer.

—Matthew Henry

The God who made the world and everything in it is the Lord of heaven and earth and does not live in temples built by hands. And he is not served by human hands, as if he needed anything, because he himself gives all men life and breath and everything else.

—Acts 17:24–25

Every good and perfect gift is from above, coming down from the Father of the heavenly lights, who does not change like shifting shadows.

—James 1:17

"Ask and it will be given to you; seek and you will find; knock and the door will be opened to you. For everyone who asks receives; he who seeks finds; and to him who knocks, the door will be opened."

—Matthew 7:7–8

"So do not worry, saying, 'What shall we eat?' or 'What shall we drink?' or 'What shall we wear?' For the pagans run after all these things, and your heavenly Father knows that you need them. But seek first his kingdom and his righteousness, and all these things will be given to you as well. Therefore do not worry about tomorrow, for tomorrow will worry about itself. Each day has enough trouble of its own."

—Matthew 6:31–34

The Lord will indeed give what is good,
    and our land will yield its harvest.

—Psalm 85:12

These all look to you
    to give them their food at the proper time.
When you give it to them,
    they gather it up;
when you open your hand,
    they are satisfied with good things.

—Psalm 104:27–28

Our Daily Bread

Do we literally ask for only bread?

We ask for *bread*; that teaches us sobriety and temperance; we ask for *bread*, not dainties, not superfluities; that which is wholesome, though it be not nice.

—Matthew Henry

The eyes of all look to you,
  and you give them their food at the proper time.
You open your hand
  and satisfy the desires of every living thing.

—Psalm 145:15–16

That evening quail came and covered the camp, and
in the morning there was a layer of dew around the
camp. When the dew was gone, thin flakes like frost
on the ground appeared on the desert floor. When the
Israelites saw it, they said to each other, "What is it?"
For they did not know what it was. Moses said to them,
"It is the bread the LORD has given you to eat." . . . Each
morning everyone gathered as much as he needed, and
when the sun grew hot, it melted away. . . . The people
of Israel called the bread manna. It was white like
coriander seed and tasted like wafers made with honey.
—EXODUS 16:13–15, 21, 31

They asked, and he brought them quail
    and satisfied them with the bread of heaven.
—PSALM 105:40

So [Elijah] did what the Lord had told him. He went to the Kerith Ravine, east of the Jordan, and stayed there. The ravens brought him bread and meat in the morning and bread and meat in the evening, and he drank from the brook.

—1 Kings 17:5–6

[The widow of Zarephath] went away and did as Elijah had told her. So there was food every day for Elijah and for the woman and her family. For the jar of flour was not used up and the jug of oil did not run dry, in keeping with the word of the Lord spoken by Elijah.

—1 Kings 17:15–16

Praise the Lord. . . .
He upholds the cause of the oppressed
    and gives food to the hungry.

—Psalm 146:1, 7

Give thanks to the Lord, for he is good.
                His love endures forever. . . .
To the One who remembered us in our low estate
                His love endures forever.
and freed us from our enemies,
                His love endures forever.
and who gives food to every creature.
                His love endures forever.
Give thanks to the God of heaven.
                His love endures forever.

—Psalm 136:1, 23–26

Keep falsehood and lies far from me;
  give me neither poverty nor riches,
  but give me only my daily bread.

—PROVERBS 30:8

Now he who supplies seed to the sower and bread for food will also supply and increase your store of seed and will enlarge the harvest of your righteousness.

—2 CORINTHIANS 9:10

"And when you pray, do not keep on babbling like pagans, for they think they will be heard because of their many words. Do not be like them, for your Father knows what you need before you ask him."

—MATTHEW 6:7–8

Late in the afternoon the Twelve came to [Jesus] and said, "Send the crowd away so they can go . . . and find food. . . ."

He replied, "You give them something to eat."

They answered, "We have only five loaves of bread and two fish—unless we go and buy food for all this crowd." (About five thousand men were there.) . . .

Taking the five loaves and the two fish and looking up to heaven, he gave thanks and broke them. Then he gave them to the disciples to set before the people. They all ate and were satisfied, and the disciples picked up twelve basketfuls of broken pieces that were left over.

—LUKE 9:12–14, 16–17

I was young and now I am old,
    yet I have never seen the righteous forsaken
    or their children begging bread. . . .
For the LORD loves the just
    and will not forsake his faithful ones.

—PSALM 37:25, 28

Our Fifth Request

And Forgive Us Our Debts
As We Forgive Our Debtors

AND FORGIVE US OUR DEBTS AS WE FORGIVE OUR DEBTORS

What does this request mean?

> We cannot plead with God to do for us what we will not do for others. Our prayer for forgiveness must, if it is real, influence our whole behavior; and if it is not real, it will not be answered.
>
> —ALEXANDER MACLAREN

> In the fifth petition, which is "And forgive us our debts, as we forgive our debtors," we pray that God, for Christ's sake, would freely pardon all our sins; which we are the rather encouraged to ask, because by His grace we are enabled from the heart to forgive others.
>
> —WESTMINSTER SHORTER CATECHISM

> "Forgive us our debts, as we also have forgiven our debtors" means, because of Christ's blood, do not hold against us, poor sinners that we are, any of the sins we do or the evil that constantly clings to us. Forgive us just as we are fully determined, as evidence of Your grace in us, to forgive our neighbors.
>
> —HEIDELBERG CATECHISM

> "And when you stand praying, if you hold anything against anyone, forgive him, so that your Father in heaven may forgive you your sins."
>
> —MARK 11:25

Be kind and compassionate to one another, forgiving each other, just as in Christ God forgave you.

—EPHESIANS 4:32

Bear with each other and forgive whatever grievances you may have against one another. Forgive as the Lord forgave you.

—COLOSSIANS 3:13

"For if you forgive men when they sin against you, your heavenly Father will also forgive you."

—MATTHEW 6:14

Forgive Us Our Debts

What are we asking God to do?

It is manifest that by debts are meant sins. The words are spoken not indeed in reference to money, but in reference to all ways in which any one sins against us, and by consequence in reference to money also.

—St. Augustine

If you, O Lord, kept a record of sins,
    O Lord, who could stand?
But with you there is forgiveness;
    therefore you are feared.

—Psalm 130:3–4

My dear children, I write this to you so that you will not sin. But if anybody does sin, we have one who speaks to the Father in our defense—Jesus Christ, the Righteous One. He is the atoning sacrifice for our sins, and not only for ours but also for the sins of the whole world.

—1 John 2:1–2

Have mercy on me, O God,
    according to your unfailing love;
according to your great compassion
    blot out my transgressions.
Wash away all my iniquity
    and cleanse me from my sin.

—Psalm 51:1–2

The LORD is slow to anger, abounding in love and forgiving sin and rebellion.

—NUMBERS 14:18

If we claim to be without sin, we deceive ourselves and the truth is not in us. If we confess our sins, he is faithful and just and will forgive us our sins and purify us from all unrighteousness.

—1 JOHN 1:8–9

Praise the LORD, O my soul,
    and forget not all his benefits—
who forgives all your sins
    and heals all your diseases,
who redeems your life from the pit
    and crowns you with love and compassion,
who satisfies your desires with good things
    so that your youth is renewed like the eagle's.

—PSALM 103:2–5

In him we have redemption through his blood, the forgiveness of sins, in accordance with the riches of God's grace that he lavished on us with all wisdom and understanding.

—EPHESIANS 1:7–8

Who is a God like you,
    who pardons sin and forgives the transgression
    of the remnant of his inheritance?
You do not stay angry forever
    but delight to show mercy.
You will again have compassion on us;
    you will tread our sins underfoot
    and hurl all our iniquities into the depths of the sea.
                                                    —MICAH 7:18–19

Then Jesus said to her, "Your sins are forgiven."
                                                    —LUKE 7:48

"For I will forgive their wickedness
    and will remember their sins no more."
                                                    —HEBREWS 8:12

As We Forgive Our Debtors

Why must we forgive others?

Christ's whole life reflected His verbal dialogue
with the Father. He did not, therefore, teach us mere
recitation. He called us into the same dialogic relationship with His Father, and then He solemnized the
relationship on the cross.

Go thou and *do* likewise.

—How, then, shall we pray the fifth petition,
"Forgive us our debts as we forgive our debtors?" Do
you see now why the asking and the acting are here so
completely connected that they cannot be separated
without violating the true praying of the Lord's Prayer?

Amen, indeed.

—Walt Wangerin

This is not a plea of merit, but a plea of grace. Note, those that come to God for the forgiveness of their sins against Him, must make conscience of forgiving those who have offended them, else they curse themselves when they say the Lord's Prayer.

—MATTHEW HENRY

Then Peter came to Jesus and asked, "Lord, how many times shall I forgive my brother when he sins against me? Up to seven times?"

Jesus answered, "I tell you, not seven times, but seventy-seven times."

—MATTHEW 18:21–22

Again Jesus said, "Peace be with you! As the Father has sent me, I am sending you." And with that he breathed on them and said, "Receive the Holy Spirit. If you forgive anyone his sins, they are forgiven; if you do not forgive them, they are not forgiven."

—JOHN 20:21–23

"Do not judge, and you will not be judged. Do not condemn, and you will not be condemned. Forgive, and you will be forgiven."

—LUKE 6:37

"So watch yourselves.

If your brother sins, rebuke him, and if he repents, forgive him. If he sins against you seven times in a day, and seven times comes back to you and says, 'I repent,' forgive him."

—LUKE 17:3–4

Our Sixth Request

Lead Us Not into Temptation but Deliver Us from the Evil One

Lead Us Not into Temptation but Deliver Us from the Evil One

What does this request mean?

In the sixth petition, which is "And lead us not into temptation, but deliver us from evil," we pray that God would either keep us from being tempted to sin, or support and deliver us when we are tempted.

—Westminster Shorter Catechism

"And lead us not into temptation, but deliver us from the evil one" means, by ourselves we are too weak to hold our own even for a moment. And our sworn enemies—the devil, the world, and our own flesh—never stop attacking us. And so, Lord, uphold us and make us strong with the strength of Your Holy Spirit, so that we may not go down to defeat in this spiritual struggle, but may firmly resist our enemies until we finally win the complete victory.

—Heidelberg Catechism

The prayer is not, that we should *not* be tempted, but that we should not be brought into temptation; as if, were it necessary that any one should be examined by fire, he should pray, not that he should not be touched by the fire, but that he should not be consumed.

—St. Augustine

Be self-controlled and alert. Your enemy the devil
prowls around like a roaring lion looking for someone
to devour. Resist him, standing firm in the faith,
because you know that your brothers throughout the
world are undergoing the same kind of sufferings.

—1 PETER 5:8–9

Finally, be strong in the Lord and in his mighty
power. Put on the full armor of God so that you can
take your stand against the devil's schemes. For our
struggle is not against flesh and blood, but against
the rulers, against the authorities, against the powers
of this dark world and against the spiritual forces of
evil in the heavenly realms.

—EPHESIANS 6:10–12

The Lord is my shepherd, I shall not be in want.

    He makes me lie down in green pastures,

he leads me beside quiet waters.

    he restores my soul.

He guides me in paths of righteousness

    for his name's sake.

Even though I walk

    through the valley of the shadow of death,

I will fear no evil,

    for you are with me;

your rod and your staff,

    they comfort me.

You prepare a table before me

    in the presence of my enemies.

Your anoint my head with oil;

    my cup overflows.

Surely goodness and love will follow me

    all the days of my life,

and I will dwell in the house of the Lord

    forever.

—Psalm 23

No temptation has seized you except what is common to man. And God is faithful; he will not let you be tempted beyond what you can bear. But when you are tempted, he will also provide a way out so that you can stand up under it.

—1 Corinthians 10:13

Lead Us Not into Temptation

What are we asking God to do for us?

> God tempts no man (James 1:13). This phrase, then, must be used in the sense of permitting. Do not suffer us, or permit us, to be tempted to sin. In this it is implied that God has such control over us and the tempter, as to save us from it if we call upon Him. The word *temptation*, however, means sometimes trial, affliction, anything that tests our virtue.
>
> —Albert Barnes

> Temptation has two parts in it—the circumstances which lead to sin, the desire which is addressed by them. There must be tinder as well as spark, if there is to be flame. Fire falling on water or bare rock will kindle nothing. God sends the one, we make the other.
>
> —Alexander MacLaren

Where does God say he will lead us?

> Who among the gods
> is like you, O Lord? . . .
> In your unfailing love you will lead
> the people you have redeemed.
> In your strength you will guide them
> to your holy dwelling.
>
> —Exodus 15:11, 13

Be strong and courageous. Do not be terrified; do not be discouraged, for the LORD your God will be with you wherever you go.

—JOSHUA 1:9

Since you are my rock and my fortress,
     for the sake of your name lead and guide me.
Free me from the trap that is set for me,
     for you are my refuge.
Into your hands I commit my spirit;
     redeem me, O LORD, the God of truth.

—PSALM 31:3–5

Lead me, O LORD, in your righteousness
     because of my enemies—
     make straight your way before me.

—PSALM 5:8

Teach me your way, O Lord;
    lead me in a straight path
    because of my oppressors.

—Psalm 27:11

Search me, O God, and know my heart;
    test me and know my anxious thoughts.
See if there is any offensive way in me,
    and lead me in the way everlasting.

—Psalm 139:23–24

Yet I am always with you;
    you hold me by my right hand.
You guide me with your counsel,
    and afterward you will take me into glory.

—Psalm 73:23–24

The Lord will guide you always;
    he will satisfy your needs in a sun-scorched land
and will strengthen your frame.
    You will be like a well-watered garden,
    like a spring whose waters never fail.

—Isaiah 58:11

Teach me to do your will,
    for you are my God;
may your good Spirit
    lead me on level ground.

—Psalm 143:10

Listen, my son, accept what I say,
and the years of your life will be many.
I guide you in the way of wisdom
and lead you along straight paths.
When you walk, your steps will not be hampered;
when you run, you will not stumble.

—Proverbs 4:10–12

"This is what the Lord says to his anointed . . .
I will go before you
and will level the mountains;
I will break down gates of bronze
and cut through bars of iron.
I will give you the treasures of darkness,
riches stored in secret places,
so that you may know that I am the Lord,
the God of Israel, who summons you by name."

—Isaiah 45:1, 2–3

"The man who enters by the gate is the shepherd of
his sheep. . . . He calls his own sheep by name and
leads them out. When he has brought out all his own,
he goes on ahead of them, and his sheep follow him
because they know his voice."

—John 10:2, 3–4

"They will neither hunger nor thirst,
nor will the desert heat or the sun beat upon them.
He who has compassion on them will guide them
and lead them beside springs of water."

—Isaiah 49:10

This is what the Lord says—
    your Redeemer, the Holy One of Israel:
"I am the Lord your God,
    who teaches you what is best for you,
    who directs you in the way you should go."

              —Isaiah 48:17

Where can I go from your Spirit?
    Where can I flee from your presence?
If I go up to the heavens, you are there;
    if I make my bed in the depths, you are there.
If I rise on the wings of the dawn,
    if I settle on the far side of the sea,
even there your hand will guide me,
    your right hand will hold me fast.

              —Psalm 139:7–10

In his heart a man plans his course,
but the LORD determines his steps.

—PROVERBS 16:9

"When Israel was a child, I loved him,
and out of Egypt I called my son. . . .
I led them with cords of human kindness,
with ties of love;
I lifted the yoke from their neck
and bent down to feed them."

—HOSEA 11:1, 4

"For the Lamb at the center of the throne will be their
shepherd;
he will lead them to springs of living water.
And God will wipe away every tear from their eyes."

—REVELATION 7:17

BUT DELIVER US FROM THE EVIL ONE

From what and from whom are we asking deliverance?

Deliver us from his power, his snares, his arts, his
temptations. He is supposed to be the great parent of
evil, and to be delivered from him is to be safe. Or it
may mean, deliver us from the various evils and trials
which beset us, the heavy and oppressive calamities
into which we are continually liable to fall.

—ALBERT BARNES

Dear children, do not let anyone lead you astray.
He who does what is right is righteous, just as he
is righteous. He who does what is sinful is of the
devil, because the devil has been sinning from the
beginning. The reason the Son of God appeared was
to destroy the devil's work.

—1 JOHN 3:7–8

"My prayer is not that you take them out of the world
but that you protect them from the evil one."

—JOHN 17:15

For I am convinced that neither death nor life,
neither angels nor demons, neither the present
nor the future, nor any powers, neither height nor
depth, nor anything else in all creation, will be able
to separate us from the love of God that is in Christ
Jesus our Lord.

—ROMANS 8:38–39

But the Lord is faithful, and he will strengthen and
protect you from the evil one.

—2 THESSALONIANS 3:3

When tempted, no one should say, "God is tempting
me." For God cannot be tempted by evil, nor does he
tempt anyone; but each one is tempted when, by his
own evil desire, he is dragged away and enticed.

—JAMES 1:13–14

The salvation of the righteous comes from the LORD;
  he is their stronghold in time of trouble.
The LORD helps them and delivers them;
  he delivers them from the wicked and saves them,
  because they take refuge in him.

—PSALM 37:39–40

Therefore put on the full armor of God, so that when
the day of evil comes, you may be able to stand your
ground, and after you have done everything, to stand.
Stand firm then, with the belt of truth buckled around
your waist, with the breastplate of righteousness in
place, and with your feet fitted with the readiness
that comes from the gospel of peace. In addition to all
this, take up the shield of faith, with which you can
extinguish all the flaming arrows of the evil one.

—EPHESIANS 6:13–16

I write to you, fathers,
>because you have known him who is from the beginning.

I write to you, young men,
>because you are strong,
>and the word of God lives in you,
>and you have overcome the evil one.

>—1 JOHN 2:14

We know that anyone born of God does not continue
to sin; the one who was born of God keeps him safe,
and the evil one cannot harm him. We know that
we are children of God, and that the whole world
is under the control of the evil one. We know also
that the Son of God has come and has given us
understanding, so that we may know him who is true.
And we are in him who is true—even in his Son Jesus
Christ. He is the true God and eternal life.

>—1 JOHN 5:18–20

Submit yourselves, then, to God. Resist the devil, and
he will flee from you.

>—JAMES 4:7

Do not set foot on the path of the wicked
>or walk in the way of evil men. . . .

The path of the righteous is like the first gleam of dawn,
>shining ever brighter till the full light of day.

But the way of the wicked is like deep darkness;
>they do not know what makes them stumble.

>—PROVERBS 4:14, 18–19

May God himself, the God of peace, sanctify you through and through. May your whole spirit, soul and body be kept blameless at the coming of our Lord Jesus Christ.

—1 Thessalonians 5:23

Grace and peace to you from God our Father and the Lord Jesus Christ, who gave himself for our sins to rescue us from the present evil age, according to the will of our God and Father, to whom be glory for ever and ever. Amen.

—Galatians 1:3–5

93

THE CONCLUSION TO THE PRAYER

FOR YOURS IS THE KINGDOM, AND THE POWER AND THE GLORY FOREVER

For Yours Is the Kingdom, and the Power and the Glory Forever

What does this conclusion mean?

He is to be "first, last, supremest, best" in our view;
and all selfish and worldly views are to be absorbed
in that one great desire of the soul that God may be
"all in all." Approaching Him with these feelings, our
prayers will be answered, our devotions will rise like
incense, and our lifting up our hands will be like the
evening sacrifice.

—Albert Barnes

The conclusion of the Lord's Prayer . . . as it stands in connection with the rest of the prayer, implies, that we desire and ask all the things mentioned in each petition, with a subordination, and in subservience, to the dominion and glory of God; in which all our desires ultimately terminate, as their last end. God's glory and dominion are the two first things mentioned in the prayer, and are the subject of the first half of the prayer; and they are the two last things mentioned in the same prayer, in its conclusion. God's glory is the Alpha and Omega in the prayer.

—Jonathan Edwards

We rejoice that *our* King reigns in providence and shall reign in grace, from the river even to the ends of the earth, and of His dominion there shall be no end.

—Charles H. Spurgeon

This means we have made all these requests of You because, as our all-powerful King, You not only want to, but are able to give us all that is good; and because Your holy name, and not we ourselves, should receive all the praise, forever.

—Heidelberg Catechism

The conclusion of the Lord's Prayer, which is "For thine is the kingdom, and the power, and the glory, forever, Amen," teacheth us to take our encouragement in prayer from God only, and in our prayers to praise Him, ascribing kingdom, power, and glory to Him.

—Westminster Shorter Catechism

Praise be to you, O Lord,
 God of our father Israel,
 from everlasting to everlasting.
Yours, O Lord, is the greatness and the power
 and the glory and the majesty and the splendor,
 for everything in heaven and earth is yours.
Yours, O Lord, is the kingdom;
 you are exalted as head over all.
Wealth and honor come from you;
 you are the ruler of all things.
In your hands are strength and power
 to exalt and give strength to all.
Now, our God, we give you thanks,
 and praise your glorious name.

—1 Chronicles 29:10–13

For Yours Is the Kingdom

What are we requesting?

> The LORD will reign
>> for ever and ever.
>>> —EXODUS 15:18

> The LORD reigns forever;
>> he has established his throne for judgment.
>>> —PSALM 9:7

> He rules forever by his power,
>> his eyes watch the nations—
>> let not the rebellious rise up against him.
>>> —PSALM 66:7

> The LORD reigns forever,
>> your God, O Zion, for all generations.
> Praise the LORD.
>>> —PSALM 146:10

> The seventh angel sounded his trumpet, and there
> were loud voices in heaven, which said:
>> "The kingdom of the world has become the
>> kingdom of our Lord and of his Christ, and
>> he will reign for ever and ever."
>>> —REVELATION 11:15

How great are his signs,
   how mighty his wonders!
His kingdom is an eternal kingdom;
   his dominion endures from generation to generation.
                                                    —Daniel 4:3

"Your throne, O God, will last for ever and ever,
   and righteousness will be the scepter of your kingdom."
                                                    —Hebrews 1:8

AND THE POWER

What power is this?

Not merely has He authority over, but He works indeed through all—the whole world and all creatures are the field of the ever present energy of God. That is a simple truth, deep but clear, that all power comes from Him. He is the cause of all changes, physical and all other. Force is the garment of the present God, and among men all power is from Him. His will is the creative word.

—ALEXANDER MACLAREN

O LORD, God of our fathers, are you not the God who is in heaven? You rule over all the kingdoms of the nations. Power and might are in your hand, and no one can withstand you.

—2 CHRONICLES 20:6

Great is our Lord and mighty in power;
    his understanding has no limit.

—PSALM 147:5

God is exalted in his power.
    Who is a teacher like him?

—JOB 36:22

The Almighty is beyond our reach and exalted in power;
    in his justice and great righteousness, he does not
    oppress.

—JOB 37:23

God is mighty, but does not despise men;
    he is mighty, and firm in his purpose.

—JOB 36:5

See, the Sovereign LORD comes with power,
    and his arm rules for him.
See, his reward is with him,
    and his recompense accompanies him.

—ISAIAH 40:10

He made the earth by his power;
    he founded the world by his wisdom
    and stretched out the heavens by his understanding.

—JEREMIAH 51:15

And the God of all grace, who called you to his
eternal glory in Christ, after you have suffered a little
while, will himself restore you and make you strong,
firm and steadfast. To him be the power for ever and
ever. Amen.

—1 PETER 5:10–11

God, the blessed and only Ruler, the King of kings and Lord of lords, who alone is immortal and who lives in unapproachable light, whom no one has seen or can see. To him be honor and might forever. Amen.

—1 TIMOTHY 6:15–16

Ah, Sovereign LORD, you have made the heavens and the earth by your great power and outstretched arm. Nothing is too hard for you.

—JEREMIAH 32:17

To him who loves us and has freed us from our sins by his blood, and has made us to be a kingdom and priests to serve his God and Father—to him be glory and power for ever and ever! Amen.

—REVELATION 1:5–6

And the Glory Forever

What does this mean?

That is, Thine is the honor or praise. Not our honor,
but Thy glory, Thy goodness, will be displayed in
providing for our wants; Thy power, in defending
us; Thy praise, in causing Thy kingdom to spread
through the earth.

—Albert Barnes

Ascribing glory to God forever, intimates an acknowledgment, that it is eternally due, and an earnest desire to
be eternally doing it, with angels and saints above.

—Matthew Henry

Who among the gods is like you, O Lord?
Who is like you—
    majestic in holiness,
    awesome in glory,
    working wonders?

—Exodus 15:11

Lift up your heads, O you gates;
    be lifted up, you ancient doors,
    that the King of glory may come in.
Who is this King of glory?
    The Lord strong and mighty,
    the Lord mighty in battle.
Lift up your heads, O you gates;
    lift them up, you ancient doors,
    that the King of glory may come in.
Who is he, this King of glory?
    The Lord Almighty—
    he is the King of glory.

—Psalm 24:7–10

Ascribe to the Lord, O mighty ones,
    ascribe to the Lord glory and strength.
Ascribe to the Lord the glory due his name;
    worship the Lord in the splendor of his holiness.

—Psalm 29:1–2

Glory in his holy name;
let the hearts of those who seek the LORD rejoice.

—PSALM 105:3

Not to us, O LORD, not to us
but to your name be the glory,
because of your love and faithfulness.

—PSALM 115:1

May the glory of the LORD endure forever.

—PSALM 104:31

Suddenly a great company of the heavenly host
appeared with the angel, praising God and saying,
"Glory to God in the highest,
and on earth peace to men on whom his favor rests."

—LUKE 2:13–14

Ascribe to the LORD, O families of nations,
ascribe to the LORD glory and strength,
ascribe to the LORD the glory due his name.

—1 CHRONICLES 16:28–29

So whether you eat or drink or whatever you do, do it
all for the glory of God.

—1 CORINTHIANS 10:31

Be exalted, O God, above the heavens;
let your glory be over all the earth.

—PSALM 57:11

"Who has ever given to God,
     that God should repay him?"
For from him and through him and to him are all things.
     To him be the glory forever!
          Amen.

—Romans 11:35–36

Shout with joy to God, all the earth!
     Sing the glory of his name;
     make his praise glorious!
Say to God, "How awesome are your deeds!
     So great is your power
     that your enemies cringe before you.
All the earth bows down to you;
     they sing praise to you,
     they sing praise to your name."

—Psalm 66:1–4

Forever

Then I heard every creature in heaven and on earth
and under the earth and on the sea, and all that is in
them, singing:
>"To him who sits on the throne and to the Lamb
>be praise and honor and glory and power for ever
>and ever!"

—Revelation 5:13

For this God is our God for ever and ever;
>he will be our guide even to the end.

—Psalm 48:14

But grow in the grace and knowledge of our Lord and
Savior Jesus Christ. To him be glory both now and
forever! Amen.

—2 Peter 3:18

To the only wise God be glory forever through Jesus
Christ! Amen.

—Romans 16:27

The word of the Lord stands forever.

—1 Peter 1:25

The Closing to the Prayer

Amen

Amen

What do we mean when we close with the word Amen?

The little word *Amen* indicates strong affirmation and means "let it be so." It expresses the faith we should have when we pray. For at the end of your prayers, you say *Amen* with heartfelt confidence and faith. When you say *Amen,* the prayer is sealed, and it will be certainly heard. Without this ending, neither the beginning nor the middle of the prayer will be of any benefit.

—Martin Luther

Amen means "this is sure to be!" It is even more sure that God listens to my prayer, than that I really desire what I pray for.

—Heidelberg Catechism

In testimony of our desire, and assurance to be heard, we say, "Amen."

—WESTMINSTER SHORTER CATECHISM

To all this we are taught to affix our *amen*, so be it. God's *amen* is a grant; his *fiat* is, it shall be so; our *amen* is only a summary desire; our *fiat* is, let it be so: it is in the token of our desire and assurance to be heard, that we say *amen*.

—MATTHEW HENRY

"If you believe, you will receive whatever you ask for in prayer."

—MATTHEW 21:22

"Therefore I tell you, whatever you ask for in prayer, believe that you have received it, and it will be yours."

—MARK 11:24

Then Jesus answered, "Woman, you have great faith! Your request is granted." And her daughter was healed from that very hour.

—MATTHEW 15:28

But when he asks, he must believe and not doubt, because he who doubts is like a wave of the sea, blown and tossed by the wind.

—JAMES 1:6

For no matter how many promises God has made,
they are "Yes" in Christ. And so through him the
"Amen" is spoken by us to the glory of God.

—2 Corinthians 1:20

Praise be to the Lord, the God of Israel,
   from everlasting to everlasting.
Let all the people say, "Amen!"
Praise the Lord.

—Psalm 106:48

Praise be to the Lord, the God of Israel,
   from everlasting to everlasting.
   Then all the people said "Amen" and "Praise the Lord."

—1 Chronicles 16:36

Ezra praised the Lord, the great God; and all the people lifted their hands and responded, "Amen! Amen!" Then they bowed down and worshiped the Lord with their faces to the ground.

—Nehemiah 8:6

Praise be to his glorious name forever;
    may the whole earth be filled with his glory.
        Amen and Amen.

—Psalm 72:19

Praise be to the Lord forever!
    Amen and Amen.

—Psalm 89:52

MORE ABOUT PRAYER

What Is Prayer?

Prayer is conversation with God.

—St. Clement of Alexandria

The Lord's Prayer (as indeed every prayer) is a letter sent from earth to heaven.

—Matthew Henry

Prayer is the work of faith alone. No one, except a believer, can truly pray.

—Martin Luther

Prayer is a sincere, sensible, affectionate pouring out of the soul to God, through Christ in the strength and assistance of the Spirit, for such things as God has promised.

—John Bunyan

Prayer is the preface to the book of Christian living, the text of the new life sermon, the girding on of the armor for battle, the pilgrim's preparation for his journey; and it must be supplemented by action or it amounts to nothing.

—Anonymous

Prayer is nothing else but a sense of God's presence.

—Brother Lawrence

Therefore, speaking comprehensively, we understand by prayer: every religious act by which we take upon ourselves directly to speak to the Eternal Being.

—Abraham Kuyper

Prayer is faith passing into action.

—Richard Cecil

Prayer can do anything God can do.

—E. M. Bounds

The possibilities and necessity of prayer, its power and results are manifested in arresting and changing the purpose of God and in relieving the stroke of His power.

—E. M. Bounds

Prayer is an offering up of our desires unto God, for things agreeable to His will, in the name of Christ, with confession of our sins, and thankful acknowledgment of His mercies.

—Westminster Shorter Catechism

Prayer is God's appointed way for obtaining things, and the great secret of all lack in our experience, in our life and in our work, is neglect of prayer.

—R. A. Torrey

WHY SHOULD WE PRAY?

God insists that we ask, not because He needs to
know our situation, but because we need the spiritual
discipline of asking.

—CATHERINE MARSHALL

Do not be anxious about anything, but in everything,
by prayer and petition, with thanksgiving, present
your requests to God.

—PHILIPPIANS 4:6

"So I say to you: Ask and it will be given to you; seek and
you will find; knock and the door will be opened to you.
For everyone who asks receives; he who seeks finds; and
to him who knocks, the door will be opened."

—LUKE 11:9–10

"Again, I tell you that if two of you on earth agree about anything you ask for, it will be done for you by my Father in heaven. For where two or three come together in my name, there am I with them."

—MATTHEW 18:19–20

The point of prayer is not to get answers from God, but to have perfect and complete oneness with Him.

—OSWALD CHAMBERS

Devote yourselves to prayer, being watchful and thankful.

—COLOSSIANS 4:2

What other nation is so great as to have their gods near them the way the LORD our God is near us whenever we pray to him?

—DEUTERONOMY 4:7

Come near to God and he will come near to you.

—JAMES 4:8

Let us then approach the throne of grace with confidence, so that we may receive mercy and find grace to help us in our time of need.

—HEBREWS 4:16

The LORD is near to all who call on him,
    to all who call on him in truth.

—PSALM 145:18

[We should pray] because prayer is the most important part of the thankfulness God requires of us. And also because God gives His grace and Holy Spirit only to those who pray continually and groan inwardly, asking God for these gifts and thanking Him for them.

—HEIDELBERG CATECHISM

How can I repay the LORD
 for all his goodness to me? . . .
I will sacrifice a thank offering to you
 and call on the name of the LORD.

—PSALM 116:12, 17

For everything God created is good, and nothing is to be rejected if it is received with thanksgiving, because it is consecrated by the word of God and prayer.

—1 Timothy 4:4–5

Speak to one another with psalms, hymns and spiritual songs. Sing and make music in your heart to the Lord, always giving thanks to God the Father for everything, in the name of our Lord Jesus Christ.

—Ephesians 5:19–20

Other reasons to pray

On reaching the place, [Jesus] said to them, "Pray
that you will not fall into temptation."

—LUKE 22:40

Answer me when I call to you,
    O my righteous God.
Give me relief from my distress;
    be merciful to me and hear my prayer.

—PSALM 4:1

Is any one of you in trouble? He should pray. Is
anyone happy? Let him sing songs of praise. Is any
one of you sick? He should call the elders of the
church to pray over him and anoint him with oil
in the name of the Lord. And the prayer offered in
faith will make the sick person well; the Lord will
raise him up. If he has sinned, he will be forgiven.
Therefore confess your sins to each other and pray for
each other so that you may be healed. The prayer of a
righteous man is powerful and effective.

—JAMES 5:13–16

Pray that the LORD your God will tell us where we
should go and what we should do.

—JEREMIAH 42:3

Then I acknowledged my sin to you
    and did not cover up my iniquity.
I said, "I will confess
    my transgressions to the LORD"—
and you forgave
    the guilt of my sin.
Therefore let everyone who is godly pray to you
    while you may be found.

—PSALM 32:5–6

WHEN SHOULD WE PRAY?

Our whole life should be a life of prayer. We should
walk in constant communion with God. There
should be a constant upward looking of the soul to
God. We should walk so habitually in His presence
that even when we awake in the night it would be the
most natural thing in the world for us to speak to
Him in thanksgiving or in petition.

—R. A. TORREY

All the time:

Pray continually.

—1 THESSALONIANS 5:17

Then Jesus told his disciples a parable to show them
that they should always pray and not give up.

—LUKE 18:1

And pray in the Spirit on all occasions with all kind of prayers and requests. With this in mind, be alert and always keep on praying for all the saints.

—Ephesians 6:18

In the morning:

In the morning, O Lord, you hear my voice;
    in the morning I lay my requests before you
    and wait in expectation.

—Psalm 5:3

Very early in the morning, while it was still dark, Jesus got up, left the house and went off to a solitary place, where he prayed.

—Mark 1:35

In the afternoon:

> One day Peter and John were going up to the temple
> at the time of prayer—at three in the afternoon.
>
> —ACTS 3:1

> Cornelius answered: "Four days ago I was in my
> house praying at this hour, at three in the afternoon.
> Suddenly a man in shining clothes stood before me."
>
> —ACTS 10:30

Three times a day:

> Now when Daniel learned that the decree had been
> published, he went home to his upstairs room where
> the windows opened toward Jerusalem. Three times
> a day he got down on his knees and prayed, giving
> thanks to his God, just as he had done before.
>
> —DANIEL 6:10

> But I call to God,
>   and the LORD saves me.
> Evening, morning and noon
>   I cry out in distress,
>   and he hears my voice.
>
> —PSALM 55:16–17

In the evening:

> And when the time for the burning of incense came,
> all the assembled worshipers were praying outside.
>
> —LUKE 1:10

> After [Jesus] had dismissed them, he went up on
> a mountainside by himself to pray. When evening
> came, he was there alone.
>
> —MATTHEW 14:23

Before meals:

> If I take part in the meal with thankfulness, why am I
> denounced because of something I thank God for? So
> whether you eat or drink or whatever you do, do it all
> for the glory of God.
>
> —1 CORINTHIANS 10:30–31

> [Jesus] told the crowd to sit down on the ground.
> When he had taken the seven loaves and given
> thanks, he broke them and gave them to his disciples
> to set before the people, and they did so.
>
> —MARK 8:6

Where Should We Pray?

Pray alone. Let prayer be the key of the morning and the bolt at night. The best way to fight against sin is to fight on our knees.

—Philip Henry

In private:

"But when you pray, go into your room, close the door and pray to your Father, who is unseen. Then your Father, who sees what is done in secret, will reward you."

—Matthew 6:6

In bed:

> On my bed I remember you;
>> I think of you through the watches of the night.
>>> —Psalm 63:6

At the river:

> On the Sabbath we went outside the city gate to the river, where we expected to find a place of prayer. We sat down and began to speak to the women who had gathered there.
>> —Acts 16:13

On the seashore:

> But when our time was up, we left and continued on our way. All the disciples and their wives and children accompanied us out of the city, and there on the beach we knelt to pray.
>> —Acts 21:5

At the well:

> Then [Abraham's servant] prayed, "O Lord, God of my master Abraham, give me success today, and show kindness to my master Abraham. See, I am standing beside this spring, and the daughters of the townspeople are coming out to draw water."
>> —Genesis 24:12–13

In God's house:

There was also a prophetess, Anna, the daughter of
Phanuel, of the tribe of Asher. She was very old; she
had lived with her husband seven years after her
marriage, and then was a widow until she was eighty-
four. She never left the temple but worshiped night
and day, fasting and praying.

—LUKE 2:36–37

On the battlefield:

On the day the LORD gave the Amorites over to Israel,
Joshua said to the LORD in the presence of Israel:
"O sun, stand still over Gibeon,
    O moon, over the Valley of Aijalon."
So the sun stood still
    and the moon stopped,
till the nation avenged itself on its enemies.

—JOSHUA 10:12–13

How Should We Pray?

We learn to pray by praying, and two concentrated
hours a day taught me much. To begin, I need to
think more about God than about myself when I am
praying. Even the Lord's Prayer centers first in what
God wants from us. "Hallowed be your name, your
kingdom come, your will be done"—God wants us to
desire these things, to orient our lives around them.

—PHILLIP YANCEY

With hands lifted up:

The ceremony of lifting up our hands in prayer is designed to remind us that we are far removed from God, unless our thoughts rise upward: as it is said in the psalm, "Unto thee, O LORD, do I lift up my soul" (Psalm 25:1).

—JOHN CALVIN

Then Solomon stood before the altar of the LORD in front of the whole assembly of Israel, spread out his hands toward heaven.

—1 KINGS 8:22

Hear my cry for mercy
    as I call to you for help,
as I lift up my hands
    toward your Most Holy Place.

—PSALM 28:2

I want men everywhere to lift up holy hands in prayer, without anger or disputing.

—1 TIMOTHY 2:8

Lift up your hands in the sanctuary
    and praise the LORD.

—PSALM 134:2

I will praise you as long as I live,
    and in your name I will lift up my hands.

—Psalm 63:4

Let us lift up our hearts and our hands
    to God in heaven.

—Lamentations 3:41

While kneeling:

When Solomon had finished all these prayers and
supplications to the LORD, he rose from before the
altar of the LORD, where he had been kneeling with
his hands spread out toward heaven.

—1 Kings 8:54

Then, at the evening sacrifice, I rose from my self-
abasement, with my tunic and cloak torn, and fell on
my knees with my hands spread out to the LORD my
God and prayed.

—Ezra 9:5

When he had said this, he knelt down with all of
them and prayed.

—Acts 20:36

Face down:

> Going a little farther, he fell with his face to the ground
> and prayed, "My Father, if it is possible, may this cup
> be taken from me. Yet not as I will, but as you will."
>
> —MATTHEW 26:39

While crying:

> In bitterness of soul Hannah wept much and prayed
> to the LORD. . . . Hannah was praying in her heart,
> and her lips were moving but her voice was not heard.
>
> —1 SAMUEL 1:10, 13

> Then the Israelites, all the people, went up to Bethel,
> and there they sat weeping before the LORD. They
> fasted that day until evening and presented burnt
> offerings and fellowship offerings to the LORD.
>
> —JUDGES 20:26

> While Ezra was praying and confessing, weeping and
> throwing himself down before the house of God, a
> large crowd of Israelites—men, women and children—
> gathered around him. They too wept bitterly.
>
> —EZRA 10:1

Hear my prayer, O LORD,
    listen to my cry for help,
    be not deaf to my weeping.
For I dwell with you as an alien,
    a stranger, as all my fathers were.
Look away from me, that I may rejoice again
    before I depart and am no more.

—PSALM 39:12–13

Hezekiah turned his face to the wall and prayed to the LORD, "Remember, O LORD, how I have walked before you faithfully and with wholehearted devotion and have done what is good in your eyes." And Hezekiah wept bitterly.

—2 KINGS 20:2–3

During the days of Jesus' life on earth, he offered up prayers and petitions with loud cries and tears to the one who could save him from death, and he was heard because of his reverent submission.

—HEBREWS 5:7

While sitting:

The King David went in and sat before the LORD, and he said:

"Who am I, O Sovereign LORD, and what is my family, that you have brought me this far?"

—2 SAMUEL 7:18

While standing:

Then Solomon stood before the altar of the LORD in front of the whole assembly of Israel and spread out his hands.

—2 CHRONICLES 6:12

And the Levites . . . said: "Stand up and praise the LORD your God, who is from everlasting to everlasting.

Blessed be your glorious name, and may it be exalted above all blessing and praise."

—NEHEMIAH 9:5

In groups:

> "Again, I tell you that if two of you on earth agree
> about anything you ask for, it will be done for you by
> my Father in heaven. For where two or three come
> together in my name, there am I with them."
>
> —MATTHEW 18:19–20

> I will give you thanks in the great assembly;
>   among throngs of people I will praise you.
>
> —PSALM 35:18

HOW DO WE KNOW GOD HEARS OUR PRAYERS?

> Prayers are instantly noticed in heaven. Our God not
> only hears prayer but also loves to hear it.
>
> —CHARLES H. SPURGEON

> Therefore this is what the Sovereign LORD says. . . .
> "Before they call I will answer;
>   while they are still speaking I will hear."
>
> —ISAIAH 65:13, 24

> The LORD appeared to [Solomon] at night and said. . . .
> "If my people, who are called by my name, will humble
> themselves and pray and seek my face and turn from
> their wicked ways, then will I hear from heaven and
> will forgive their sin and will heal their land."
>
> —2 CHRONICLES 7:12, 14

"Then you will call upon me and come and pray to me, and I will listen to you."

—Jeremiah 29:12

We know that God does not listen to sinners. He listens to the godly man who does his will.

—John 9:31

Surely then you will find delight in the Almighty
    and will lift up your face to God.
You will pray to him, and he will hear you,
    and you will fulfill your vows.

—Job 22:26–27

The Lord is far from the wicked
but he hears the prayer of the righteous.

—Proverbs 15:29

You hear, O Lord, the desire of the afflicted;
you encourage them, and you listen to their cry.

—Psalm 10:17

The righteous cry out, and the Lord hears them;
he delivers them from all their troubles.

—Psalm 34:17

Does God Answer Our Prayers?

If our petitions are in accordance with His will, and
if we seek His glory in the asking, the answers will
come in ways that will astonish us and fill our hearts
with songs of thanksgiving. God is a rich and bounti-
ful Father, and He does not forget His children, nor
withhold from them anything which it would be to
their advantage to receive.

—J. Kennedy Maclean

Then you will call, and the Lord will answer;
    you will cry for help, and he will say: Here am I.
—Isaiah 58:9

[Hannah said to Eli] . . . "I prayed for this child, and
the Lord has granted me what I asked of him."
—1 Samuel 1:26–27

If any of you lacks wisdom, he should ask God, who
gives generously to all without finding fault, and it
will be given to him.

—James 1:5

"In that day you will no longer ask me anything. I tell
you the truth, my Father will give you whatever you
ask in my name. Until now you have not asked for
anything in my name. Ask and you will receive, and
your joy will be complete."

—John 16:23–24

Dear friends, if our hearts do not condemn us, we have confidence before God and receive from him anything we ask, because we obey his commands and do what pleases him.

—1 John 3:21–22

Before Isaiah had left the middle court, the word of the Lord came to him: "Go back and tell Hezekiah, the leader of my people, 'This is what the Lord, the God of your father David, says: I have heard your prayer and seen your tears; I will heal you. On the third day from now you will go up to the temple of the Lord. I will add fifteen years to your life.'"

—2 Kings 20:4–6

This is the confidence we have in approaching God: that if we ask anything according to his will, he hears us. And if we know that he hears us—whatever we ask—we know that we have what we asked of him.

—1 John 5:14–15

"Therefore I tell you, whatever you ask for in prayer, believe that you have received it, and it will be yours."

—Mark 11:24

"If you believe, you will receive whatever you ask for in prayer."

—Matthew 21:22

What Are the Elements of Godly Prayer?

Praise

> Praise is begotten by gratitude and a conscious obliga-
> tion to God for mercies given. Praise is so distinctly
> and definitely wedded to prayer, so inseparably joined,
> that they cannot be divorced. Praise is dependent on
> prayer for its full volume and its sweetest melody.
>
> —E. M. Bounds

> At that time Jesus said, "I praise you, Father, Lord of
> heaven and earth, because you have hidden these things
> from the wise and learned, and revealed them to little
> children. Yes, Father, for this was your good pleasure."
>
> —Matthew 11:25–26

> Praise be to the God and Father of our Lord Jesus
> Christ! In his great mercy he has given us new birth
> into a living hope through the resurrection of Jesus
> Christ from the dead.
>
> —1 Peter 1:3

Thanksgiving

> Thanksgiving is just what the word itself signifies—
> the giving of thanks to God. It is giving something
> to God in words which we feel at heart for blessings
> received. Giving thanks is the very life of prayer.
>
> —E. M. Bounds

Always giving thanks to God the Father for
everything, in the name of our Lord Jesus Christ.

—Ephesians 5:20

And whatever you do, whether in word or deed, do
it all in the name of the Lord Jesus, giving thanks to
God the Father through him.

—Colossians 3:17

Give thanks in all circumstances, for this is God's
will for you in Christ Jesus.

—1 Thessalonians 5:18

Petition

> Whether we like it or not, asking is the rule of the kingdom.
>
> —Charles H. Spurgeon

> "Ask and it will be given to you; seek and you will find; knock and the door will be opened to you. For everyone who asks receives; he who seeks finds; and to him who knocks, the door will be opened."
>
> —Matthew 7:7–8

Confession

> The preparation of proper prayer is the plea for pardon with a humble and sincere confession of guilt. Nor should anyone, however holy he may be, hope that he will obtain anything from God until he is freely reconciled to Him.
>
> —John Calvin

> If we confess our sins, he is faithful and just and will forgive us our sins and purify us from all unrighteousness.
>
> —1 John 1:9

Then I acknowledged my sin to you
    and did not cover up my iniquity.
I said, "I will confess
    my transgressions to the LORD"—
and you forgave
    the guilt of my sin.

—PSALM 32:5

Intercession
We intercede for others:

A frequent intercession with God, earnestly beseeching Him to forgive the sins of all mankind, to bless them with His Spirit, and bring them to everlasting happiness, is the divinest exercise that the heart of man can be engaged in.

—WILLIAM LAW

I urge, then, first of all, that requests, prayers, intercession and thanksgiving be made for everyone—for kings and all those in authority, that we may live peaceful and quiet lives in all godliness and holiness.

—1 TIMOTHY 2:1–2

Therefore confess your sins to each other and pray for each other so that you may be healed. The prayer of a righteous man is powerful and effective.

—James 5:16

While they were stoning him, Stephen prayed, "Lord Jesus, receive my spirit." Then he fell on his knees and cried out, "Lord, do not hold this sin against them." When he had said this, he fell asleep.

—Acts 7:59–60

So Peter was kept in prison, but the church was earnestly praying to God for him.

—Acts 12:5

Christ intercedes for us:

Prayer in the name of Christ has power with God. God is well pleased with His Son Jesus Christ. He hears Him always, and He also hears always the prayer that is really in His name. There is a fragrance in the name of Christ that makes acceptable to God every prayer that bears it.

—R. A. Torrey

"And I will do whatever you ask in my name, so that the Son may bring glory to the Father. You may ask me for anything in my name, and I will do it."

—John 14:13–14

"In that day you will no longer ask me anything. I tell you the truth, my Father will give you whatever you ask in my name."

—John 16:23

But because Jesus lives forever, he has a permanent priesthood. Therefore he is able to save completely those who come to God through him, because he always lives to intercede for them.

—Hebrews 7:24–25

My dear children, I write this to you so that you will not sin. But if anybody does sin, we have one who speaks to the Father in our defense—Jesus Christ, the Righteous One.

—1 John 2:1

What Should We Say When We Pray?

"Two men went up the temple to pray, one a Pharisee
and the other a tax collector. The Pharisee stood up
and prayed about himself: 'God, I thank you that I am
not like other men—robbers, evildoers, adulterers—
or even like this tax collector. I fast twice a week and
give a tenth of all I get.' But the tax collector stood at a
distance. He would not even look up to heaven, but beat
his breast and said, 'God, have mercy on me, a sinner.'

I tell you that this man, rather than the other,
went home justified before God. For everyone who
exalts himself will be humbled, and he who humbles
himself will be exalted."

—Luke 18:10–14

"And when you pray do not keep on babbling like
pagans, for they think they will be heard because
of their many words. Do not be like them, for your
Father knows what you need before you ask him."

—Matthew 6:7–8

In the same way, the Spirit helps us in our weakness.
We do not know what we ought to pray for, but the
Spirit himself intercedes for us with groans that
words cannot express.

—Romans 8:26

"This, then, is how you should pray:
Our Father in heaven,
hallowed be your name,
your kingdom come,
your will be done
    on earth as it is in heaven.
Give us today our daily bread.
Forgive us our debts,
    as we also have forgiven our debtors.
And lead us not into temptation,
but deliver us from the evil one.
[For yours is the kingdom and the power and the glory
    forever.
    Amen.]"

—Matthew 6:9–13

Sources

Barnes, Albert. *Barnes' New Testament Notes.* Christian Classics Ethereal Library. www.ccel.org.

Bounds, E(dward) M. *Essentials of Prayer.* Christian Classics Ethereal Library. www.ccel.org.

Bounds, E(dward) M. *Necessity of Prayer.* Christian Classics Ethereal Library. www.ccel.org.

Bounds, E(dward) M. *Purpose in Prayer.* Christian Classics Ethereal Library. www.ccel.org.

Calvin, John. *Institutes of the Christian Religion.* Christian Classics Ethereal Library. www.ccel.org.

Calvin, John. *Of Prayer—A Perpetual Exercise of Faith, The Daily Benefits Derived from It.* Christian Classics Ethereal Library. www.ccel.org.

Chambers, Oswald. *My Utmost for His Highest.* James Reiman, ed. ©1992 Oswald Chambers Publication Association, Ltd, Discovery House, Grand Rapids, MI.

Edwards, Jonathan. *The Works of Jonathan Edwards, Volume 1.* Christian Classics Ethereal Library. www.ccel.org.

Gill, John. *Doctrinal Divinity, Book 1.* Christian Classics Ethereal Library. www.ccel.org.

The Heidelberg Catechism, copyright 2006, Christian Reformed Church in North America, Grand Rapids, MI.

Henry, Matthew. *Commentary on the Whole Bible, Volume V (Matthew to John).* Christian Classics Ethereal Library. www.ccel.org.

Kuyper, Abraham, *Work of the Holy Spirit; Essence of Prayer.* Christian Classics Ethereal Library. www.ccel.org.

Luther, Martin, *Faith Alone.* James C. Galvin, ed., ©1998, 2005 by James C. Galvin. Used by permission of Zondervan.

MacLaren, Alexander. *Expositions of Holy Scripture: Ezekiel, Daniel, and the Minor Prophets; and Matthew Chapters I to VIII.* Christian Classics Ethereal Library. *www.ccel.org.*

Mead, Frank S., ed., *12,000 Religious Quotations.* Grand Rapids, MI: Baker Publishing Group, 1989.

Schaff, Philip. NPNF1–06. *St. Augustine: Sermon on the Mount; Harmony of the Gospels; Homilies on the Gospels*. Christian Classics Ethereal Library. www.ccel.org.

Spurgeon, Charles Haddon. *Morning and Evening: Daily Reading*. Christian Classics Ethereal Library. www.ccel.org.

Spurgeon, Charles Haddon. *Spurgeon Sermon Collection, Volume 1*. Christian Classics Ethereal Library. www.ccel.org.

Torrey, R(euben) A(rcher). *How to Pray*. Christian Classics Ethereal Library. www.ccel.org.

Watson, Thomas. *Lord's Prayer*. Christian Classics Ethereal Library. www.ccel.org.

Wesley, John. *Wesley's Notes on the Bible*. Christian Classics Ethereal Library. www.ccel.org.